D1526371

Brew The Beer : Learn The Business of Brewing

Alcohol, Volume 1

Rocoo Martin

Published by MINDPOP, 2020.

While every precaution has been taken in the preparation of this book, the publisher assumes no responsibility for errors or omissions, or for damages resulting from the use of the information contained herein.

BREW THE BEER : LEARN THE BUSINESS OF BREWING

First edition. May 9, 2020.

Copyright © 2020 Rocoo Martin.

ISBN: 978-1393555438

Written by Rocoo Martin.

Table of Contents

ABSTRACT

As the market demand for craft brewed beer continues to grow, small brewers are continuing to crop up to meet the demand. The increasing number of small breweries also comes from an increasing number of brewery closings—over 80 since 2010. While they can master the brewing process fundamentals with little technical knowledge, the key to a prosperous brewery is optimizing the use of all resources, especially considering rising energy costs. Recent brewing operations often have the choice between building their own facility from scratch, or contracting their brewing operations to an established facility. This project recommends a design for a craft brewery producing varieties of beer with a 100,000 bbl/year total production capacity. The recommended design minimizes the use of external utilities by maximizing the heat integration of process streams. I performed a rigorous economic analysis to determine the profitability of the process design. The startup and operations costs for building an independent facility following this design were calculated, and from this a reasonable rate for contract brewing was determined. I found it that the construction of an independent facility would require a total permanent investment of $68MM and have a net present value (NPV) of $26MM with an internal rate of return (IRR) of 20.96% in the present year. To achieve the same returns, it was determined that contract brewing would only be a more economically viable option if the contracted production price is less than $8.72/gallon of beer.

CHOOSE A NAME

If you're of an age to enjoy craft brews like me, you probably have been to your fair share of small breweries. Between the interior, the vibes, the music, the food, the staff, and the craft, a standout name is also key.

Some of my favorite names include Hop Dogma (California), Fat Head's (Portland), Triple Voodoo (San Francisco), Alpha Acid (Belmont)—and those are all local! The possibilities are endless. What makes a significant brewery name?

Enjoy choosing from this list of inspiration. Experiment with the sortable lists. When choosing a name, think about the theme of your brewery:

- Is it nature-oriented, trendy, traditional, or funky?
- What type of people do you want to attract?
- What is your expertize—what inspired you?
- Where are you located?
- What makes your craft brews unique?

We list some examples below:

- Ether Brew Co.
- 8 Ball Brewing
- Final Days Brew Co
- 7th Heaven Brewing
- Snake Eyes Brewing

- The Blue Dog Brewery
- Blue Ocean Bottle works
- El Diablo's Brewing
- The Mistress
- Candle Wick
- Space Age
- Alpha Beta
- Cold Break
- Nitrogen Brew Co.
- Drishti Brew Co.
- The Reaper Brewing Co.
- Black Magic Brew Co.
- Cedar Cider Works
- Jet Black Brewing
- Nickel and Yeast Brewing
- Blue Skye Brewing Co.
- Apple and Pear Brewing
- Madrone Brewing
- Dusty Bottle Brewing
- Cottonwood Bottlers
- Everest Brew Co.
- Red Jasper Brew Co.
- Cherry and Plum Brewing
- True Cedar Brew Co.
- Ale House
- [Local River]
- Ale House
- [Local Mountain]
- Brewery
- [Local Geographic Feature]
- Brewing Company
- [Founder Name]

- Pour House
- [Street Name]
- Ales
- [Family Member's Name]
- Fine Ales
- [Local Cove]
- [Local Beach]
- Ales and Lagers
- [Local Team]
- [Plant Name]
- Barrel
- [Constellation Name]
- [Yeast Strain]
- [Club Name]
- [Inspirational Word]
- [Favorite Noun]
- [Favorite Adjective]
- Beerology

FORM AN ENTITY

Business use serves two principal purposes:

(1) it protects your personal assets from the debt of your new company; and

(2) where you have multiple owners, clear and unpleasant agreements between owners who they are, what rights each of the owners have, and what happens if the owner wishes to leave, helping to reduce disputes.

Most business owners prefer any company with limited credit and a Subchapter S Corporate form for their business. Using LLCs or companies can be a valuable tool for planning and protecting business owners' assets, and many attorneys can build these assets at a reasonable cost in a brief period.

Before you get to the fun part of making beer, it's important to take the right legal steps to start your own business. The first step in this is to choose the right business structure for the business. Business choice involves several observations, including debt securities, taxes, capital formation and management. This article summarizes the business structures and related issues to consider.

Facilitation of the State

Real ownership is the only automatic ownership when one owner runs a business. The processing of the soliloquy is simple and rarely requires a filing by state authorities. All income and business losses are reported directly by the owner. However, new producers should think twice before relying on this simple form of ownership. Matter alone does not enjoy credit protection. Instead, providers are solely responsible for all debts and claims against the business. If it only related it was only to an unexpected claim, the owner's assets could be at risk.

A partnership

Collaboration is the default form of ownership when over one owner runs a business. A standard collaboration would be possible without the formal filing by the two groups performing at the concert. In a general partnership, all partners may take action on behalf of the partnership and share the debt of collateral with the claims. Alternatively, the parties may establish a limited partnership by completing a certificate of limited cooperation with the applicable federal authorities. Through limited partnerships, the general partner has the authority to act on behalf of the partnership and is responsible for the debt of the partnership. A limited partner is usually an investor with no management rights and enjoys limited liability. The partnership includes a tax return of the information and the affiliates report their allocated share of the partnership's income and losses.

Limited Liability Company

A limited liability company (LLC) is probably the most common entity dealing with alcohol sales. This is because the LLC offers greater flexibility in the importance of business management and capital formation. The

LLC provides limited liability its members reports to each of its members and. The LLC is formed by completing the articles of association with the applicable state authorities. Members will wish to establish a working agreement for establishing management and business economics.

Organization

A corporation is a legal entity formed under state law by completing articles of incorporation of applicable state authorities. The organization releases shares to its participants, who then enjoy limited credit protection. An organization can be the preferred form of business to generate momentum expecting to find limited investors (as some investors wish to invest in the organization only). The key return on operating as an organization is that the business is subject to a "double taxation," meaning that the company pays taxes and its participants pay a second tax rate on the distribution from the corporation. The organization can avoid this double taxation, but only if it makes an "S" election. In that case, the income and loss of the corporation are reported directly by the shareholders. The "S" option requires certain filings with the IRS and is subject to significant restrictions regarding its financial structure.

More thoughts

Offenders may rent or purchase property. If the manufacturer of the pool owns the real property, they should a separate business entity that operates the real property. This structure provides an additional level of credit protection (although tax consequences should be based on individual facts and circumstances). A real estate agency (which is likely to be an LLC) can lease your property to a running business.

After selecting the structure for your business, the requirements for completing and managing the business do not end there. Businesses usually have to find the taxpayer identification number of the organization and will be subject to tax. When an entity uses employees, it must also consider the employment tax and compensation structures of its employees. It should also follow corporate management should also, which may include a partnership agreement, operating agreement or stock agreement (subject to a business appointment), annual minutes and authorization decisions.

FILE A TRADEMARK FOR YOUR BREWERY NAME

A trademark is any individual or combination of words, phrases, symbols or designs that identifies or distinguishes the source of goods of one party from those of another. A service mark does for services what a trademark does for goods. Trademarks protect the goodwill that owners create to identify goods and services, not the goods and services themselves. Trademarks can also exist indefinitely (subject to ongoing use and renewal requirements).

Registering a trademark or service mark begins by applying with the USPTO. The USPTO uses attorneys who will review the application for proper legal and procedural grounds. Most times, the examining attorney responds to the application with an "office action." The attorney highlights any conflicts with the proposed mark, or any other objections to granting registration in the office action. The applicant responds to any conflicts or problems noted in the office action within six months. After six months, if the applicant does not respond, I deem the application "dead." If the application either receives no objections for registration, or if the applicant overcomes any objections within the six-month period, the USPTO publishes the mark for opposition. Any party who may contest the registration of the mark must do so within 30 days of the publication date. If no one contests the mark, then the USPTO will register the mark, typically 12 weeks following the publication date. Once you select a mark, the overall USPTO process from start to finish averages between 12 and 18 months.

Careful trademark and service mark management can lead to a successful brand development and increase the value of a company or product. However, use and registration of trademarks and service marks can be a complicated and treacherous landscape. The knowledge of an experienced attorney can help navigate the terrain of trademark law, and lead to an outcome of branding success.

File Trademarks for Your Beer Names

With new craft breweries launching every day, the competition for beer names is fierce. Once you select the names and design logos, you need to file trademark for these as well (NOTE: if you have your beer names selected at the time you apply for a Federal trademark for the brewery name you can submit the applications for the beer names at the same time–up to 36 months before the launch of the beer itself).

LEASE A SPACE

As in the old cliché, real estate is about "location, location, location," and this is especially true for the brewing business. If you are looking for a neighborhood brewery, you will need to find a suitable location close to home. If you have big ambitions, you can look for a more strategic position to expand later. Whatever it is, you must save space to complete the licensing process.

The new brewery owner first leases the building and negotiating the lease is an important step.

Commercial lease agreements usually have one of two types: "triple net" and "gross."

In the triple net, the tenant pays the landlord a pro-rated share of the rent, taxes, insurance and operating expenses. In a typical triple net lease, the tenant pays a fixed amount of basic rent every month, and taxes, insurance and maintenance costs (also known as CAM, or common area), plus an "extra lease" for maintenance costs. At the end of the lease year, we compare the estimated amounts to the actual costs and are adjusted based on whether the tenant pays more or less by their monthly payments.

In a "gross" lease, the landlord agrees to pay all costs associated with ownership. The tenant pays a certain amount each month, nothing more.

1) Alcohol required

1.1. Utilities.

The first thing we learn about commercial space is to quickly determine the volume of water, sewer, electricity and gas supply (or at least the building) coming into the unit. Breweries are essential for all these utilities and it is very expensive to upgrade. It is important to know these facts about the place before submitting the offer.

Check these utility requirements with specific mechanical systems. The water main diameter should be at least two inches and the sewer led 4 inches. In a multi-tenant building, the water supply per unit may be smaller than the water main for the building. As long as the main body of the building is large enough, install a large water main for the entire building (for example, k 5K versus $10- 50K for the new main), rather than the cost of running the new water line from the main floor of the building.

Tip: If the sprinkler system is already installed in the building, then the water and wastewater supply in the building is sufficient.

Gas supply is not expensive to upgrade, and we have found that most commercial buildings already supply enough gas. If you don't plan an all-electric small brewery (10 barrels or fewer), you'll use plenty of natural gas for a steam boiler or kettle burner.

Three-phase electrical power is commonly used for brewing equipment. This provides a more consistent flow of electric motors (such as pumps and flakes). For brewery alone this should be at least 200-400 amps. Our initial build out called for 9,000 square feet of brewery and 800 amps in the taproom space. It is possible to achieve this with a single phase power for small brewing systems, but most equipment manufacturers require three steps.

They use this heavy power in most industrial buildings, although it is not yet installed in the building. Even if the building already has a neighboring tenant, you may need to implement a new 3-step service in your unit. We have learned about it. Disappointing. The cost of upgrading electricity from the nearest three-phase power grid to the building's distance is $5-50K.

1.2. Fire suppression.

Some local codes require fire extinguishers for breweries. If you have a dream plan and want it open to the brewery, you usually need to have a sprinkler system.

Without a sprinkler system, fire-rated walls that separate the furnace and taproom are needed. The cause is fire.

1.3. LOADING DOCK.

It's helpful to have access to a loading dock, although not required. The requirement that will be delivered at the time of installation, breweries receive frequent deliveries of materials. If a dock isn't available, a drive-in door and forklift will suffice.

If the building has a shared loading dock, verify actual usage among the current tenants and if there are any restrictions to the hours, we can use it.

1.4. TAPROOM NEEDS.

1.4.1. RESTROOMS.

Taprooms have higher occupancy ratings, so we require more restroom stalls (which, you guessed it, means a higher cost to build). For example, our taproom occupancy will be less than 200 people, but our local code calls for three stalls for four men and three stalls for women.

Unless you're looking at a former high occupancy space, you will probably build more/larger restrooms. We do not design industrial and warehouse buildings for high occupancy so will have very few restroom facilities.

Tip: Large mixed-use (warehouse + office) buildings sometimes have common-sized common toilets that are shared by the build-

*ing's tenants. This is a big bonus if you have easy access to the pa-
trons of your position and have enough done.*

2) PARKING

Along with the higher occupancy of a taproom come higher parking requirements. Local code varies on specific parking requirements depending on how your establishment is classified. Even if the local code doesn't
require much dedicated off-street parking, consider how your location
will affect customers driving to visit the taproom. If there's consistently
not enough parking and most people drive in your area, customers may
avoid visiting.

*Tip: Even if a multi-tenant building seems to have a lot of abundant park-
ing, all the spots may already be allocated by code to existing tenants based
on their type of business and occupancy rating. Increasing the occupancy of a
unit may cause a deficit of parking spots according to local code.*

2.1. ACCESSIBILITY.

As retail business open to the public, be aware of ADA codes regarding
how accessible your establishment must be to people with disabilities.
This has implications to restroom design, height of ordering/pick up
counters, parking spots, and several accessible entrances and exits.

*Tip: If entrances and exits are not at ground level, ADA-compliant ramps
and/or lifts may need to be installed.*

3) LOCATION AND ZONING

Typically, breweries are only allowed in industrially zoned districts, but some cities are loosening regulations around this. Brew companies that don't produce are sometimes allowed in more traditional business districts similar to restaurants.

Learn about your local zoning regulations before starting your search for a building. It is sometimes possible to receive a zoning exemption from a city, but this is usually a lengthy application process combined with public hearings. It's best to stick to looking within zones where a brewery is already permitted, if possible.

Tip: Contact the area's zoning or planning office directly to verify a building is in a zone that permits your type of brewery with no special exemption.

4) LEASING CONSIDERATIONS

4.1. LANDLORD ATTITUDE.

It is better to find a place with a brewery-friendly landlord. We've discovered that building owners fall into one of four categories:

Will not consider a brewery tenant under any circumstances.

Will allow a brewery but not a taproom (usually just concerned about liability of the public drinking alcohol on premises).

Open to having a brewery and taproom (hey, if you're willing to pay, they're willing to lease it).

Super pumped about having a brewery/taproom tenant (will go above and beyond to help).

After having encountered these types, we love #4 the best and found that in our current landlord. You'll be making major changes to their building and will need their help more than you probably think, so it's important to have a landlord that supports your business and responds to your requests.

Tip: Think of the landlord like a business partner—what qualities are important to you?

4.2. LEASE RATE AND EXPENSES.

We'll publish a more detailed article about leases later on, but here are the basics. We structure commercial lease rates in one of the follow ways:

Gross Rent = total rent including tenant's share of building operating expense and property taxes (often also includes the utilities)

Triple Net (AKA changed gross) = three net rents comprising (1) the base rent; (2) tenant's share of property operating expense; and (3) tenant's share of building property taxes.

The property's operating expenses are often abbreviated as "CAM", or "common area management."

Unlike residential leases, which are advertised as the total monthly rent amount, they typically express commercial rental rates are typically in price per square foot per year. This is what I mean when a commercial broker says the price is $X a foot. To calculate how much it will cost per month, multiply the rate by total square feet and then divide by 12 months.

Example: $8 per foot for a 2,500 square foot unit.
   ($8 x 2,500) / 12 = $1,666.67 per month
   If a 10,000 square foot unit is advertised as "$10 per foot gross", this unit costs $100,000 per year in rent but includes CAM and taxes.

A 10,000 square foot unit is advertised as "$10 per foot net-net". This means the base rent is $100,000 per year and doesn't include CAM and net tax expenses. We will express the CAM and taxes as a per square foot rate, but can increase or decrease year-to-year (usually increase).

Tip: Always ask whether it includes the CAM and taxes in the rental rate if it's not clear. Commercial properties advertised as $X per month rarely include CAM/taxes, which makes it appear at first glance like a great bargain.

4.3. TENANT IMPROVEMENTS (TI)

Since businesses have so many unique real estate requirements and often sign multi-year leases, it's common for landlords in retail or mixed-use buildings to offer a credit towards part or all of the build-out expenses. Some landlords even have their own construction crews to perform the work on behalf of the tenant.

Some landlords offer TI loans that are structured into the lease payments. Provided the interest rate and terms compete with traditional bank loans, this is an excellent way for a business to fund the build-out.

Tip: The cheaper the rent and shorter the term, the less likely a landlord will offer a TI credit or loan. TI credit is often negotiated rather than advertised as a specific amount, such as "Will Build to Suit".

LICENSE AND AGREEMENT REQUIREMENT

Have Your Brewer and Other Key Employees Sign Employment Agreements

Most employees in Minnesota and other states are "at will" employees; this is the reason when they can quit their job, for whatever reason. If the employer of the business has a key employee integral to its success, the employee must have a written employment contract that provides employment for a specified period. A key employee may include non-compete agreements to leave the job for a competitor. The chief employee may leave, except in this contract.

A written employment agreement is a must for your head brewer, who knows that brewery principles can cause much damage to a competitive business. Therefore, the master brewer must not compete and contract with the employment contract, and the terms expressly state that beer principles are "trade secrets" and are therefore the property of the brewery.

Agreements should be narrowly adopted without competing to balance the interests of the employer and employee. The employer must show (i) that we must not accept the agreement when the agreement is signed (if the test of the agreement is the continued employment of the employee, we must sign the agreement before the valid employment begins); (ii) protects the legitimate business interest of the Covenant Owner; (iii) The Covenant is reasonable in geographical scope to protect the employer with no prior burden on the right of the former employee to survive.

1) If you are raising funds, be subject to federal and state security laws

Finding suitable financing for a startup venture like a new brewery is difficult. Many startup brewery operators are resorting to private funding sources for their recent venture.

When soliciting private funds, we must follow federal and state security laws. The definition of "security" is very broad and is not limited to stock shares. This includes partnership and LLC interests, promissory notes and many other financing instruments. Securities must be registered or exempt from state and federal law registration requirements. If some written disclosure and information is made available to investors or made available to them, they may have sufficient information to make investment decisions. Focus on "accredited investors," who have a net worth of a million dollars excluding their home. The disclosure requirements for these advanced investors are minimal. However, even if you are exempt from registration, there will still be liability for any fraud by the issuer.

The consequences of not complying with federal and state security laws are severe and may include administrative, civil, and criminal penalties. Therefore, before seeking private financing for your new brewery, be sure to consult with knowledgeable persons and be eligible to handle security matters.

2) Apply for your brewer's notice with TTB

Maintaining and maintaining your own brewery is an important - and time-consuming - process of licensing the brewery from the Bureau of Alcohol and Tobacco Trade and Tax
(TTB). The TTB wants federal excise taxes on alcohol, tobacco, firearms and ammunition and guarantees it complies
with federal tobacco permits and alcohol permits, labeling
and marketing requirements to protect consumers.

If you want to brew beer for family or personal use, the TTB
must approve your activities, recipes, beer labels. You need
to send in the brewer's notice and have a brewer's bond, and
the TTB must approve their operations before brewing the
beer. TTB may begin an on-site inspection of the proposed
premises and operations before your brewer gives notice. It also requires background checks on directors, officers and significant employers. This process usually takes 6–12 months to
complete.

3) Apply for Applicable State and Local Licenses

Besides the TTB approval, the new brewery must apply for a state wholesaler's license and any license required by the municipality to operate the
brewery. The next example is the taproom license. In Minnesota, they
can purchase beer pins on-site at the brewery if the brewer intends to
build and operate the toilet license, the municipality must issue which
rather than the state of Minnesota.

To make sure you get these licenses in the first place, you need to put a
checklist of factors that will help you get these licenses. Here is a list that
you can put on the last minute to avoid discrepancies.

- Power commercial power line

- Commercial Waterline - Municipality / Underground Bore Water

- Registration Land Registration / Lease Approval

- Company registration

- Poll is a waste disposal certificate from the Pollution Control Board

- Quality of equipment manufactured

MACHINERY REQUIREMENT

We have listed the essential set of equipment that you must run your business smoothly. In case you are adding a microbrewery to your existing restaurant, you may also use the existing infrastructure for it.

The equipment that you would need in a brewery would be a separate water tank, water softener machine, a RO machine setup, and separate fermenters. Other types of equipment that you may require are mentioned below.

- Mashing tuns and Kettles
- Refrigeration machine
- PHEs (Physical Heat exchangers)
- Electric Cabinet
- Beer Filters
- Boiler
- Distribution Tanks
- PLC touch-type process controller
- Serving System
- Lauter Tuns
- Fermenters

For genuine lovers of craft beer, starting a company can be the ultimate dream. What better business to start with friends making something you love for you and other beer enthusiasts?

In fact, many people are passionate about brewing beer. According to the Home brewers Association, there are about 1.1 million Home brewers in the U.S., producing over 1.4 million barrels of beer in 2017. The number of enthusiasts who are turning their brewing hobbies into breweries continues to grow. The Brewers Association counted 6,266 craft breweries in the U.S. in 2017, a 15.5 percent increase from the year before.

From Hobby to starting a Brewery

Making the start from a home operation to starting a full-fledged brewery business can be a challenge. Any small business idea takes plenty of planning, money, and perseverance to become successful. But starting a brewery requires large, expensive, specialized equipment, along with the know-how and space to operate it. There are also legal and permitting issues unique to the industry to consider.

Finding Your Equipment

The cost of equipment can vary depending on many things, such as the quantity of beer you wish to produce and whether you want to purchase new or used. Your startup budget will often determine the size and age of the equipment you buy. When starting a brewery, your equipment list will need to include kettles, boilers, fermentation tanks, filters, cooling systems, storage tanks, kegs, bottling or canning equipment, refrigeration, piping, and cleaning tools. Acquiring equipment for restaurants covers some same issues.

Equipment List for starting a Brewery with price

1) Brew House

A brew company contains of all the essential equipment's, or vessels, a craft brewery needs for the initial brewing stage. It typically includes a mash mixer, lauter tun, tropical liquor tank, holding kettle, boil kettle, and whirlpool. A two-vessel brew house is often made up of combinations of a mash mixer/lauter tun/tropical liquor tank and boil kettle/whirlpool, while a larger, more advanced five-vessel system separates these components.

The first step is to extract liquid from the mashing of malt and other grains. We then move this is then to the kettle where it's boiled with hops or other ingredients, producing the flavor, color, and aroma of your beer. At the conclusion of the boil, it separates the wort settles in the whirlpool out.

Pricing for a Brewhouse

Brewery equipment maker SS Brew tech has developed brew house at different capacities, with prices ranging from just under $50,000 for a 3.5-barrel (bbl.) system to $98,500 for a 20 bbl system.

2) Fermentation and Brite Tanks

The next step in the beer-making process—and the next item that should be on your equipment list—takes place in the fermentation tank, with yeast feeding on the wort to produce alcohol and carbonation. This makes it one of the most important pieces of equipment for any person starting a brewery. Consider tanks with a cone-shaped bottom, allowing the yeast to be easily captured and removed for later use. These gleaming stainless-steel vats are also one of the largest and most prominent pieces of brewing equipment, sometimes prominently displayed behind the bar at brewpubs.

After the brewing process is complete, the beer is filtered and pumped into a secondary brite tank. Similar in looks to a fermentation tank, the brite tank allows the beer to further mature, clarify, and carbonate before we bottle it, canned, or kegged. The beer can also be served directly from the brite tank.

Pricing for Fermentation and Brite Tanks

Stout Tanks and Kettles specializes in equipment for small breweries, offering tanks in a range of sizes, both jacketed and non-jacketed. Jacketed containers allow for simple temperature control. Fermenters start at just over $2,000 for a 3 bbl. Size, while brite tanks run from just under $1,400 to over $5,500.

3) Kegs and Keg Washers

Whether you bottle your beer when starting your brewery, kegs are an essential component for storing, serving, and selling your finished product.

A keg can be tapped for your own brewpub, or sold to bars or restaurants for counter sales to customers.

Like the rest of your brewery equipment, it's vital to keep your kegs clean, to prevent spoilage or poor-tasting beer. Depending on the volume of your brewery, an automated keg washer will offer greater cleaning efficiency and lower labor costs, while helping speed up your brewing process.

Pricing for Kegs and Keg Washers

Several companies supply standard 1/2-barrel kegs, such as Beverage Factory, which sells 15.5-gallon beer kegs for $125. For keg washing systems, Portland Kettle Works offers several automated keg washes that range from just under $10,000 to over $14,000.

Establishing Craft Beer Pricing

Besides producing excellent beer, successfully starting a brewery requires setting the right price for your line of brews. Not only does the price have to be fair in customers' eyes, but it has to take into account the full cost of producing your beer, while also paying down debts and turning a profit. Unreasonable price can hurt sales; too low and you may struggle to cover expenses.

According to Craft Beer Restaurant, when selling your beer in a restaurant or brewpub, a general formula is to take the wholesale cost of your bottle of beer and multiply by 2.0 or higher (up to 3.0). Thus, a 12-ounce bottle of beer that costs you $2.50 to brew can be sold for $5 to $7 to customers.

For draught beer poured from a keg, costs are typically about 40-45 percent less per ounce than the same beer in a bottle. Use the multiplier of 2.0 or more to figure your price. But because draught beer comes with added overhead costs to store and serve, such as regular cleaning, spillage, and spoilage, it's important to add a per-glass charge to cover these extra costs.

SPACE REQUIRED TO SETUP THE FACTORY

How big should my brewery be? How many square feet do I need for a brewery? How large of a facility should I get? As the host of a podcast about how to start a brewery, I have spoken with over 70 brewers, brewery owners, and other experts in the craft beer industry. So I often hear this question from listeners around the world.

You need to consider several factors to determine the size of your brewery. For example:

- Size of your brew system
- Your annual production capacity
- Barrels of beer you plan to brew each year

Just the business model plays a major role in deciding how many square feet you'll need for your brewery.

- Brewpub serving only on-site consumption

- Nano brewery with taproom and no distribution

- Production brewery with complete bottling, canning, and kegging lines

As you could imagine, there is no one-size-fits-all size requirement. It's a tough question to answer, but an important answer to find out.

If your rule is too low, it will fill the space.

"We did not expect the need for cold storage or for a large breeding program," said Patty Elliot of Pecan Street Brewing in Johnson City, Texas.

"Although we have a sizeable building, we have brief space for Sean [underground] to keep the keys inside and we have four working tanks. So, the work tanks have to be low enough to stop, that they will fit into the store, so they can brew another beer. So we always fight the war ... and we long to find the coldest winter."

And if your purchase is too large, you are contributing significant amounts to the initial cost of the unused square cost.

However, with the explosive growth of beer that doesn't seem to slow down soon, you will expand operations as soon as you open.

When MCB Brew founder, Joe Shelerud asked the 6.1-liquor sales staff at the end of 2013, "Do you wish you knew before starting your own beer?" Around 20% of the answers were that they should have planned their expansion from the start.

"I would build a lot of infrastructure in the beginning," said Brett Tate of the Dust Bowl Brewing Company. We have been up and running on three power generation since its inception in 2009.

The requirements for a brewery space vary

If you read books about starting alcohol and online forums, you can find magic formulas to tell you how big your money-making business should be.

For example:

One thousand square feet, each barrel of standard construction 1 to 1.5 feet, each barrel produced per year.

The JVNW website has more information and detailed brochures and resource requirements. As a manufacturer of coffee making machines, they work with a wide variety of materials for many types of configuration.

JVNW-sized recommendations are:

Absolute dissolving: 0.5 to 1 square feet per container for annual capacity

Stored malt storage: 0.15 to 0.25 square feet, each capacity bar per year

Also, a few things will affect the space requirements of your writing and editing. For example:

The size and number of vessels for sale

Size and several cruise ships & sparkling tanks

How many batches do you plan to do each week?

Meanwhile, JVNW claims that the average workforce is 0.75 workers per 1,000 barrels of capacity per year. While Lakewood Brewing, which raises about 1,000 square meters per barrel for construction, has 22 employees to produce about 10,000,000,000 barrels. So about 1.76 workers out of every 1,000 jars - they double what JVNW recommends.

So, my only assumption is that the math varies.

Space requirements for breweries on Microbrewer Podcast

To get a handle on exactly what the square footage requirement is for a small craft brewery, Microbrewer Podcast listened, and Akhilesh Pandey dug into the stats from the show notes.

Another podcast listened, Peter Stillmank from Stillmank Brewing Co. in Green Bay, Wisconsin, asked for these stats to get a better picture of our discussions in microbreweries Podcast. At episode 41, I started asking for specific statistics including: size of the brewhouse, number of vessels, annual capacity, and square footage.

For this exercise, we were concerned only with it requires how many square feet for a small craft brewery.

So Akhilesh dug into the numbers and plotted them into a spreadsheet. He compared each brewery's annual capacity to its square footage and calculated the square footage per barrel of yearly capacity.

What were the results?

Well, we looked at the data from 20 different breweries from all over the U.S. plus one 1 in Ireland. (We had to leave out a few dues to incomplete data.) Models include everything from a tiny Nano brewery in the basement of a hotel, to a large production brewery with international distribution, and everything in between. We've spoken with Nano breweries, brewpubs, and production packaging breweries.

If we take the total square footage for all breweries and divide it by the total yearly capacity of all breweries, it equals 0.8 square feet required per barrel of yearly capacity. This gives sort of industry-wide efficiency, but it doesn't really look at what each brewery is doing individually.

Craft beer is a young industry. Its home to a wide variety of players with varying levels of experience, knowledge, and preferences. So the range of their space efficiency is wide.

When we calculate the square footage per barrel of yearly capacity at each individual brewery, the maximum was 40 square feet; the minimum was 0.2 square feet, and the average (mean) was 4.6 square feet per barrel.

Square footage per barrel of yearly capacity at 20 craft breweries in the U.S.A. and Ireland:

Calculation method	Square feet per yearly barrel production capacity
Maximum	40.0
Minimum	0.2
Average (mean)	4.6
Median	1.6
STD Dev. with 99% confidence	2.16
Range	39.8

That seemed kind of high. I thought maybe the average was being skewed by outliers.

So, I checked the median. The median is 1.6 square feet per barrel of yearly capacity.

Median is often used to calculate skewed data sets. It sorts of cancels out those outliers like the non-breeder that uses a whopping 40 square feet per barrel produced, and the brewpub/production brewery that somehow blasts out a full barrel of beer for every 0.2 square feet they occupy.

Now, I'm not a mathematician, I recall little from Statistics class. But Akhil has more insight to offer.

"The average the way you have it there," he writes by email, "is not the right method because it does not eliminate the outlier."

Akhil looked at the "standard deviation" (I remember that term from Statistics class) and found that those few data points that are just so far from the others, don't really help us. They're considered oddballs. By taking off the 3 outliers from the end, Akhil can get 99% confidence in his calculation.

With 99% confidence, we can guess that your brewery would need 2.16 square feet per barrel of yearly capacity.

So, there you have it

How much space do you need for your brewery in planning or for your next expansion brewery?

First figure out how many barrels of beer you plan to produce per year, your total capacity.

Then figure on needing about 2.16 square feet per barrel of yearly capacity.

STEP-BY-STEP MANUFACTURING

The ingredients used for beer making have a great bearing on the last product —— quality and quantity of each and how they are used during the process. The essential ingredient for beer making is: -

Water: - Water makes up about 90% of the finished beers. We must find out the biological purity and mineral content at the water. In brew parlance water is called liquor. We assume hard water to be better suited for lager beers whereas soft water is more ideal for heavier beers. Some mineral like Gypsum aids in separation of husk from malt results in clean finished beer. Again, mineral like natural Calcium are suited for beers. Ideally majorities of the world's breweries either change or directly use naturally available water to suit their needs.

Grain: - The most desirable and frequently used grain for making beer is top quality barley. We use varieties of Hordeum sativum. It flavors barley over other as it contains essential enzymes like Diastase and Maltase. After receiving the barley screened and cleaned. Then it is taken to malting shed and steeped in water. The grains are turned regularly to ensure contact with oxygen. Then the grain germinates as essential enzymes convert the complex starch into fermentable soluble sugar (Maltose, Dextrin etc. Malting is a process by which starch content of grain is brought to maximum. At this stage we place the Green malt on the floor of a KLIN and heat stops the process of germination but allow the enzyme Diastase to remain active. We roast the temperature of the kiln and length of time that malt determines color and sweetness of beers.

Adjuncts: - sometimes at the time of mashing malt I mixed with other cereals (rice & corn) which are frequently referred to as adjuncts. More the adjunct, lighter the body and flavor of finished beer. However, in certain countries like Germany use of adjuncts is legally banned. This one we consider the reasons for German beers to be purest of all.

Hop (Hamulus Lupulus): - Hops are a member of nettle family. It is a perennial flowering vinc. The cone shaped female flower are used for it contains "Lupulin" a bitter dust which contains tannin, resins and other essential oils. It produces the best English hop in Kent, Sussex & Worcestershire. The Bohemian hops from Czechoslovakia are amongst the world's bet. A few examples of well-known hops are: - saaz (Chez rep.) Bouillon (U.S.A), Golding & Fuggles (U. K), Hallertan (Germany).

We use hops because: -

Flavoring: - It provides the characteristic flavor

Taste: - It provides certain bitterness

Antiseptic: - Prevent microbial actions and bacterial spoilage during brewing process

Cleaning: - It is used to filter wort to remove much of sediment and solids (spent hops may be further used as fertilizer)

Clarification: - Tannin present in hops acts as clarifying agent

Preservation: - It increases shelf life of beers.

Sugar: - Specially graded and refined sugar is used that aids in a fermentation process and also give sweetness to beer. The yeast acts on sugar, therefore breaking it up into alcohol and carbon dioxide.

Yeast: - It is a microscopic unicellular microorganism that multiplies itself by cell division. The function of yeast in the beer making process is to encourage wort to ferment. The two basic varieties of brewer's yeast are:

- Saccharomyces cerevisae (also called top fermenting yeast) and Saccharomyces carlbergenises (also called bottom fermenting yeast). The co2 thus produced may not escape, but stored. The quality and quantity of yet is strictly maintained which affect the quality of beers.

Additives:- Several breweries use natural and chemical substances called additives to serve the following purpose: -

- **Peptones** :- to stabilize foam head

- **Gum Arabic** :- to stabilize foam head

- **Ascorbic acid** :- to prevent oxydation of beers which may cause loss of flavor and color

- **Hydroxybenzonate** :- acts as preservative

- **Caramel** :- to adjust color

Finnings:- Ingredient that are used to clarify beers by example: - Ising glass (swimming bladder of sturgeon fish), eggshell, peptin, etc. The findings attract the unwanted particles at the bottom of the cask, leaving the beer clear. Different filters like cellulose, asbestos etc. are also used for the same purpose.

Primings: - It is an optional process in which a solution of hops and cane sugar added to some beers (like mild ales & stout) during storage. the function of primings is to cause seconday fermentation by allowing the remaining yeast to react with the ugar producing alcohol and carbondioxide in the cask itself. this result in slightly sweeter beer.

SPECIAL NOTABLE TERM: -

Lautering: - The mash is passed to the lauter tun (with a slated base) & is stirred with movable rakes. When the stirring stops, the solid settles at the bottom and get filtered through the slated bottom. The liquid I now called wort.

Brewing: - The mash flow out to the brewing kettle, called the copper. Hops are now added, and it boils mash for 1 to 2 1/2 hrs. Sometimes while preparing brown ale and a sweet stout invert sugar and hops are added to increase amount of fermentable sugar in the wort. The boiling sterilizes, the beer and sweet stouts; invert sugar & we add hops that prevent the beers from spoilage. The process is called brewing.

Hop-Back: - After completion of brewing operation, they do hop back. This is removing spent hop in a large tank with perforated floors. The hot wort I piped into this & spent hops settle at the bottom. The wort passe through this filter of spent hops, leaving the floating oils behind.

Lagering: - This is a derivative of German word: "Lagern" meaning to store. The young beer is run off to storage vats & temperature is brought down. Though only bottom fermented beer is called lager beers, even Ale needs Lagering or maturing for a few days for proper conditioning.

Krausening: - We introduce some breweries to the beer to add zest and carbonation before they send it for lagering. This process is called KRAUSENING in German, meaning "foam" or "froth". It is used to stimulate secondary fermentation during lagering of lager type beer.

Pasteurization: - The French scientist Louis Pasteur introduced this method. We usually carry it is usually out in case of bottled or canned beer to increase shelf life. We heat the final containers with hot water spray to 60*C/140*C for at least 20min. The process kills any bacteria and any remaining yeast present in the beer, which stops secondary fermentation, which otherwise might cause an explosion of bottles & bulging of cans.

Bruised Beer: - From brewery to bar, a constant temperature is essential to maintain the quality of beer. A beer that has been warmed and cooled again suffers loss in quality and is termed as bruised beer.

TYPES OF BEER

Lager beer: -Lager is the generic term for all bottom-fermented beers. Lagting of beer takes place at a near freezing temperature. It may last from several weeks to several months. Lager beers compared to ale. Take a longer period to mature, have a less pronounced hop flavor & (except for some contrasting examples) have low alcoholic content. Lagers are light bodied. Brand names are-;

There are unique styles of lager beers, which are:

Pilsner Hie name derived from the classic Pilsner-Urquell made in town of Pilsen in Czechoslovakia.

This style of beer is a lively. Dry. Light–bodice, light! Pale golden amber colored beer. The alcohol content is 4-5% by volume. We always serve Pilsner is always chilled. Some brand names arc Slaudicr Pils. Konig-Pilsncr (Germany). Cascade (Canada) and Hcinckcn Pilsner (Holland).

Bock: - Bock beers arc traditionally strong. dark lagers with a high alcohol content & a rich malty flavor, produced in Havana. Germany, though most of them arc dark, they may also be pale or amber or bronze. The alcohol content is 6% by volume & the arc served slightly chilled. Bock beers were originally brewed seasonally to celebrate special occasions.

Double Bock: - It was originally produced by Italian monks and traditionally served as warming beers. The strongest beer in the world is a double bock called "Kulminator" (13.2% by volume), produced in Bhavana, Germany.

Light Beer: - The variant of Pilsner style beer caters today's health conscious crowd. These beers typically have 100 calories or fewer per 12 ounce serving and alcohol content of (3.2-3.9%) by volume. Brands are-Miller light, Coors Light, bud light.

Malt liquor: - They are lager beer with high alcoholic content than pilsner — - 5.5 to 6% by weight. Adding extra enzyme to increase fermentation usually produces them. Has light malt flavor. Brands–Colt 45.

Steam Beer: - It combines the bottom fermentation of lager beer with higher fermenting temperature of Ale. Alcohol content 5% by volume.

Dry beer: - This introduced in Japan in 1987. They are less sweet, lively & refreshing with little or no after taste.

Ale Beer: - Ale is a generic term for top fermented beer. It ferments ale at a higher temperature & takes less time to mature. More pronounced hop flavor, heavy body & in most cases high in alcoholic content. We do not serve them chilled.

The various styles are a follow: -

- **Cream Ale**: - Golden in color, mild beer with sweet taste.

- **Pale Ale**: - Straw colored brew made from lightly roasted malt. It has pronounced yeast and hop flavor. Alcohol content 5% by volume. Brand names: - Martin Pale Ale, Courage's Strong Pale Ale (U.K.)

- **Indian Pale Ale**: - Contains extra hop. Brand names: - Bass, Cherington's, Indian Pale Al.

- **Bitter Ale**: - Copper Colored, low in alcohol, heavily hopped, full-bodied, malty and most of them are bitter. Alcohol content — 3.5–5% by volume. Brand — Master Brew bitter, Pedegree bitter Ale (U.K.) Fuller's.

- **Mild Ale**: - Dark amber brew with sweet after taste of caramel. Lightly hopped. Alcohol content (2.5–3.5%). by volume. Brands–Mild Ale, Hanson Mild (U. K)

- **Brown Ale**: - Often referred to a "dessert wine" owing to its extra sweet taste. Alcohol content (6-12%). by volume. Brands–Provsie (Belgium), Samuel Smith (U. K)

- **Barley wine**: - Few old ales which are matured for 2 years or more. Alcohol content (3-6%). Brand–White bread's Gold label.

- **Porter**: - Light black colored beer, ha more malty and less hop flavor, wetter than stout, also called "Light Gravity Black Beer". Alcohol content (5-7.5%). Brands–Burton Porter (U. K), Sierra Nevada (U.S. A)

- **Stout** :- commonly called "Black beer", High hop content and powerful malt taste, Alcohol content (4-10%). Brands–Courage's Velvet stout, (U. K), Güines (Ireland)

Wheat Beer : - Also called "White beer". It is too fermented, a high percentage of wheat -60%, often laced with fruit, and cherished as summer drink. Brand—- Welsse, Weizanbier (Germany), Lambic, Gueze (Belgium)

Non-Alcoholic Beer — These are made either by removing the alcohol after brewing or by stopping the fermentation process before the alcohol forms; has a low calorie count; alcoholic content le than 0.5%

<u>STEP-BY-STEP PROCESS</u>:

Step 1: Milling the grain

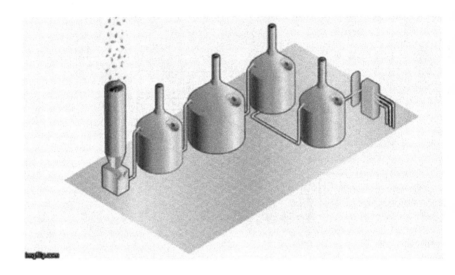

Beginning In the brewhouse, different malt are crushed together to break up the grain kernels to extract fermentable sugars to produce a milled product called grist.

Step 2: Mash Conversion

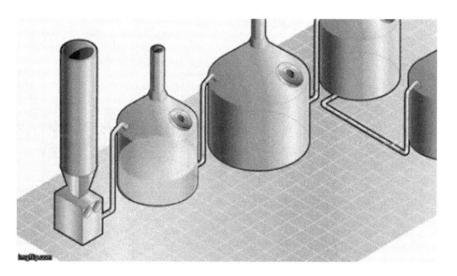

We then transfer the grist is then into a mash tun, where it is mixed with heated water in a process called mash conversion. The conversion process uses natural enzymes in the malt to break the malt's starch down into sugars.

Step 3: Lautering

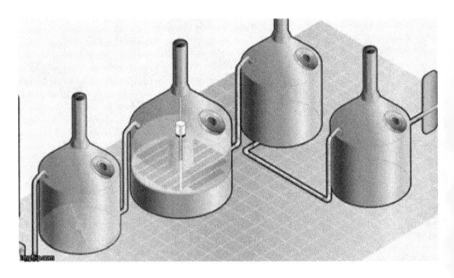

It then pumps the mash is then into the lauter tun, where a sweet liquid (known as wort) is separated from the grain husks.

Step 4: The boil

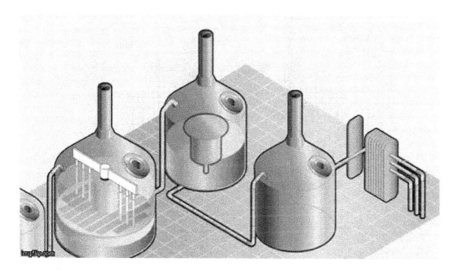

We then collect the wort is then in a vessel called a kettle where it is brought to a controlled boil before we add the hops.

Step 5: Wort separation and cooling

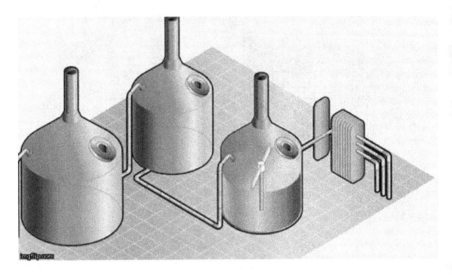

After boiling, we transfer the wort into a whirlpool for the wort separation stage. During this stage, any malt or hop particles are removed to leave a liquid ready to be cooled and fermented.

Step 6: Fermentation

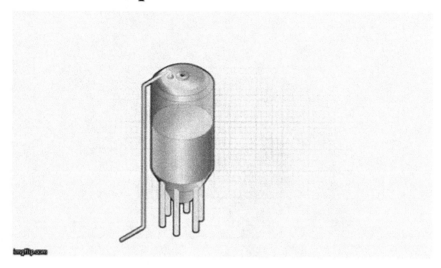

To start the fermentation, we add yeast during the filling of the vessel. Yeast converts the sugary wort into beer by producing alcohol, a wide range of flavors, and carbon dioxide (used later in the process to give the beer its sparkle).

Step 7: Maturation

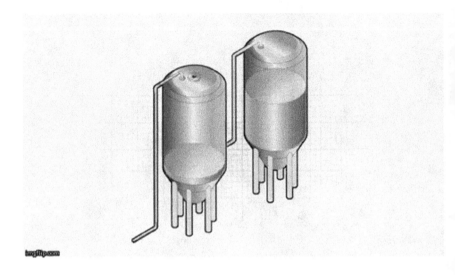

After fermentation, the young "green" beer needs to be matured to allow both a full development of flavors and a smooth finish.

Step 8: Filtration, carbonation, and cellaring

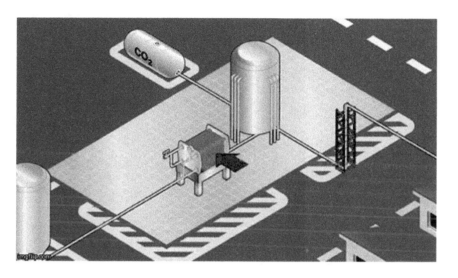

After reaching its full potential, the beer is filtered, carbonated, and transferred to the bright beer tank, where it goes through a cellaring process that takes 3-4 weeks to complete. Once completed, the beer is ready to be a package.

Beer Processing Flow Diagram

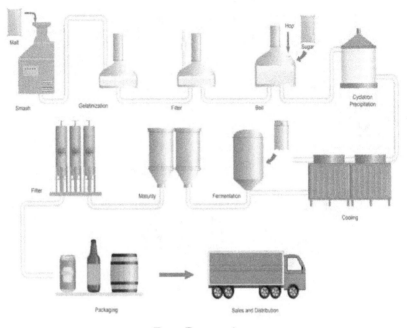

Beer Processing

PACKAGING OF BEER: -

1) **Bottled or Canned**: - Beer is manufactured at a much lower temperature. Pasteurized for longer shelf life. There should be stored at 70*F & preferably in a gloomy room. Approx. shelf life is from 3 to 6 months Bottles should be kept upright so that beer does not come in contact with the "crown seal". We can do the desired chilling before actual service.

2) **Draught Beer**: - Most draught beers are unpasteurized. So, to prevent over carbonation and souring, we must keep them under refrigeration at (36-38) ° F. The keg should have the storage area close to the bar. Secondary fermentatio0n takes place inside the keg.

DISTRIBUTION OF BEER

Three "tigers" of the program contain:

Manufacturer (a. k. a. manufacturer or supplier) tier. Beer - breeds for brewing beer, milk, and / or packaging beer. Every plumbing installation from the largest Anheuser-Busch / InBev to the smallest number falls to the manufacturer. Most observers also include importers on the producer's side, even though the line between the importer and the distributor is very narrow, especially among the small importers of Special beers.

Distributor (a. k. a. wholesaler) tier - These companies can range from "mom and pop" businesses that run a small truck shop and a few trucks to large multinational operations that sell millions of cases a year.

Shoplifter - This includes various businesses, often separated by "real estate" dealers (ie, liquor is dispensed at merchant's yards), such as liquor stores, supermarkets and so on, "on-premises" vendors (i.e. liquor used in merchant's yards), such as bars, bars. Restaurants, hotels and more.

In a three-tier distribution system, the brewery makes beer, sells it to distributors, and distributors deliver and sell beer to retailers. We, the beer-loving community, then buy from a retailer.

The three-phase system requires that all beers (and other liquor in most cases) pass through the intermediary, called a distributor (also called a dealer in other provinces). The distributor sells and sells the produce on the ground, and distributors sell the beer to retailers.

The three-lane system introduces "middle class" alcohol distribution

The plan means that beer producers do not sell directly to bars, liquor stores, or grocery stores. It is the job of the distributor to establish sales relationships. The distributor may not buy space on the shelf or apartheid, provide equipment such as cool coolers, provide loans or create a sense of obligation, or offer discounted retail prices. They should provide sellers with the same price. Distributors also keep refrigerated storage facilities for beer, and truckloads of beer to transport beer around the state.

Producers (Breweries)

Distributors

Retailers (bars, liquors stores and grocers)

Consumers (you)

Traditionally, there has been a three-tier program regarding beer distribution. In this system, a liquor company sells beer to a retailer, and sells it to a customer. Usually, small but growing domestic companies do not have the right volume for effective profit while working with distributors, many turning to using them to sell their product.

But when do you know which model of distribution is the right choice for your own making of alcohol? Distributing and distributing both have their advantages and disadvantages depending on the size of your drinking plan and strategy.

Self-Distribution

For many breweries, self-distribution offers the advantage of better margins on their product being able to get feedback directly from retailers and their consumers and they have more control of their product and where it is sold.

Self-Distribution Allows Your Brewery to:

1) Improve Margins by Cutting Out the Middleman

When your brewery sells a product to distributors, those distributors are advertising your products and shipping them to other regions. They are also a business trying to make a profit, and that time taken on your products costs them money, which they ask from you as a percentage of your profit. When your brewery can distribute your beer locally through hiring salespeople, your brewery withholds more profit compared to working with distributors because your brewery keeps all the profits from sales.

2) Have Complete Control of Your Beer

When your brewery self-distributes, you have a lot more control of how and where it is sold since your salespeople work for you. If you want to make a change of process or want your beer to be sold at a specific location, your salespeople can make that change quick. With distributors, once you sell them your product, the distributors determine how and where your beer is sold.

3) Get Feedback Directly from your Customers

With your salespeople going door-to-door, they get 1-on-1 time with your customers. They can get feedback directly from the source which is something your brewery might miss out on if you distribute with a distributor.

Limitations of Self-Distributing:

1) Self-Distribution Requires a High Capital Investment Upfront

To self-distribute, you need the following resources to start:

- Salespeople to push your product
- Vehicles & gas to get your product from place-to-place
- Equipment like forklifts and pallet jacks
- Warehouse space

Many of these resources can add up to hundreds of thousands of dollars to start. And even if you take a loan out on this equipment, there's not a guarantee your brewery will make up the capital costs if retailers don't buy your product. Your brewery must do thorough research to ensure that you can pay off the capital costs associated with self-distributing.

2) Self-Distribution Maybe Illegal in your State

Self-distribution of alcoholic beverages is legal in 36 states, but if you are in the following 14 states, it is still illegal to self-distribute:

- Alabama
- Delaware
- Florida
- Georgia
- Kansas
- Kentucky
- Louisiana
- Mississippi
- Missouri
- Nebraska
- Nevada
- Rhode Island
- South Carolina
- Vermont

In these states, using a distributor to sell your beer is the only option to expand your business.

Using Distributors

The traditional three-tiered distribution system still has many advantages compared to self-distribution depending on your brewery's size and sales strategy. Using distributors puts the responsibility of distributing and expanding your sales to them, leaving your brewery to spend time on growing the business.

Using Distributors Allows your Brewery to:

1) Rely on your Distributors' Expert Knowledge of the Market

When you partner with a distributor to sell your beer in a different region or state than your headquarters, they know the ins-and-outs of the local market and have important connections. You can rely on them to find the businesses where your beer can create and fulfill market demand.

2) Focus on the Core of Your Business

With your distributors focused on distributing your beer, your brewery can get time back to focus on crafting your brewery's business strategies. You can focus on what your brewery wells: creating innovative products and experiences for your customers.

3) Quickly Grow Your Business

If you have the right distributors in strategic regions, your brewery can grow more quickly than if you self-distributed. Because of your distributors' long-lasting relationships, they can get your beer in retail locations your brewery would have a hard time getting in on your own. And the more locations they sell your beer, your brewery has a better chance of building a customer-base nationwide.

Limitations of Utilizing Distributors

1) Using Distributors Cuts into your Margins

Distributors are still a business and will need to take a cut off your own profits to make a profit themselves. Because of this, your earnings potential lesson by utilizing a distributor compared if you self-distributed your own beer. According to Matt Robinson from Shelf Life, distributors usually require 20-30% of your beer's total margin.

2) Your Brewery Has Less Control

Once your beer is sold to a distributor, they have complete control of where and how your beer is sold in the agreed upon region. If you want to specialize the selling process or sell your beer in a certain retail establishment, that is not up to you; it is the distributor's choice.

3) Your Beers Can Get Lost in the Shuffle

Many distributors handle hundreds if not thousands of brands. Just because you have signed a contract with a distributor doesn't mean that the distributor will prioritize your brands and get them on store shelves. If your brands are not their highest sellers, they may not give your brands a fair chance to sell.

Which Method of Beer Distribution is Right for Your Brewery?

An increased profit margin sounds great, but there are some drawbacks to choosing to distribute yourself. Startup costs are higher when choosing to do things on your own. You are paying upfront to the labor for delivery equipment and warehouse space. It may limit breweries to the local market only to keep the profit margin high.

Another factor for breweries is gaining shelf and tap space, which can be tough in this competitive market. Distributors typically have contracts to secure a certain amount of space, which can be a problem when trying to get your beer into some shelf space.

Distributors often take a higher margin between 20-30%, and just because you partner with a distributor, it doesn't mean that the distributor will prioritize your brand for shelf space.

When deciding to distribute, it's important to think long term and not just in the immediate future. There is an increased profit margin with self-distribution, but are you looking to distribute out-of-state in the long run? If the answer is yes, it's important to weigh the future potential benefits of a distributor. It's also important to know that typically once you sign a distributor contract, it lock you into it, so weigh your options fully before making that decision.

MARKETING TIPS

The secret's out, everyone: today's consumers can't get enough craft beer. In the past decade, the craft brewery industry has exploded. From 2008 to 2018, indie brewers went from producing 8.5 million barrels of beer to 26 million, according to reports. In that same time period, the number of craft breweries went from 1,500 to over 7,000 in the U.S.

With the industry landscape more popular (and competitive) than ever, marketing is a tried-and-accurate way to make your brewery stand out. These nine tips will help you develop a powerful marketing strategy, no matter your budget.

1) Get noticed on social media

If you're only posting up-close shots of your latest canned variety or your open hours, you're not leveraging social media platforms as best you can. People follow companies on social media because they want to stay on top of the latest news developments and get a glimpse of the ethos behind the brand.

Sure, maybe your beer is refreshing, but what's the process for naming a new one? What does your brewery space look like? Who are the people working hard behind the scenes? Your social media pages are grand places to put all this on display while staying true to the aesthetic of your company's branding. (And, if you've got even a bit of a budget, turn some of those high-performing posts into targeted social ads to attract new fans.)

2) Partner with local businesses

Industry vets know that word of mouth is one of the most effective marketing tools around. Widen your organic reach by partnering with local restaurants and businesses. This doesn't just mean they stock your beer at their establishment, although that's a big plus. You can get creative, like offering to "sponsor" their next enormous event or fundraiser by donating some beer or offering a discount.

If you also host events at your brewery, you can consider partnering with local vendors for a preferred vendor program. This way, you can refer these businesses to clients for an event at your venue and vice versa.

3) Be active in your community

The odds are that your city has a plethora of community events happening on any weekend, whether it's an outdoor festival, a weekly food truck park, or something in between. Check out your local alt-weekly paper, chamber of commerce calendar, or coffee shop message board and see what events are coming up.

You can add a note on these dates in your Gather event calendar for team awareness. Then reach out to the coordinators and see if they still need vendors or sponsors. Even if it's too late to take part, you can still keep these annual events on your radar to make sure you've got a booth, a keg, or a cooler at them the next time around.

4) Focus on what makes you unique

There are a ton of craft breweries dotting the landscape these days. The secret to success? Standing out. Do you work with local artists on label designs, or use a rare ingredient for your summer ale? Boom, there's your angle. But even if you don't have one obvious factor that sets you apart, that doesn't mean you're out of luck.

Like we said before: people flock to brands that show their human side. Think about the journey to create your craft brewery. There's almost no chance the road was identical to someone else's every step of the way. That makes you unique, and it's worth touting.

5) Launch a newsletter

We get it: running a brewery takes serious time, and you don't have a lot to spare. But attempting to create a brief newsletter, even if you only send it once a month, can have a major impact on your business. (Case in point: For every $1 spent on email marketing, it makes approximately $32 to $44 in return.)

There are a few tactics that'll help ensure your newsletter is successful. First, think about what you want to say, and what you think readers want to know about. Even if you don't have a big recent release to announce, you can refresh readers about your latest offerings. You can also include info about tour options and keep people posted on where they can buy your beers around town. Make the subject line catchy (but appropriate). Don't forget to include all your social media links at the bottom. Last, add hyperlinks in case people want to know more about anything you mention.

CONCLUSION

The overall design for building a mid-size brewery capable of producing 100,000 barrels/year with the specified requirements: produces 10,000 barrels minimum of IPA, Imperial, Stout, Pilsner, and Lager; 4 seasonal varieties of Sour Cherry Wheat, Summer Ale, Oktoberfest, Winter Ale; and 4 limited edition offerings of Aged Imperial IPA, Oaked IPA, Extra Special Bitter, and Belgian Triple is profitable with an IRR of 20.96% and NPV of $26MM in present year. By the third year of operations, when the plant goes into full-scale production, the return on investment (ROI) will reach 15.09%, a healthy annual return. This shows that the option of building an independent facility is a viable option with IRR 20.96% > 15%, the standard corporation hurdle rate. This assumes a total permanent investment cost of $68MM and 15-year MACRS depreciation using the half-year convention for depreciation. To determine a competitive price point for contract brewing, we need the same return on investment (15.09% annually) but with none of the capital investment or tax benefits of depreciation. Based on the same sales volume of 100,000 barrels/year at $16/gallon wholesale price, this means a contract option will offer the same return on investment annually at a production price of $8.72/gallon of beer. This assumes that the development additional outside costs of 35% the total sales volume, besides the costs of production including: an extensive marketing budget, discount pricing to enter the market and gain shelf space, and additional costs outside the facility. This also assumes that consumers would still be willing to pay a premium wholesale price of $16/gallon for beer that was produced in a contract brewing facility.

Recommendation

71

Based on these calculations, we recommend the company move forward building the facility if they can complete the project within our budget and design specifications. If they can get a contract price lower than approximately $8.72/gallon—then contract brewing becomes a viable alternative. The sensitivity analysis show that we are insensitive to the price of ingredients and utilities; however, our profit margin is sensitive to changes in equipment cost or capacity requirements. This means that once we invest in the plant and complete it on budget, profits are not threatened by external pricing factors. The contract brewing option eliminates the upfront risk of building an entire facility for an untested new brand and product. The detailed design report shows the pros and cons of building a new facility and the contract brewing option. Our recommendation is to bid out a contract for brewing with a contract brewing facility, if bids come in below $8.72/gallon of beer, and then contract brewing becomes a competitive option vs. building a new facility and the pros and cons of contract brewing should be further explored.

About the Author

Rocco Martin is a lifestyle enthusiast and author of multiple books and articles on travel & lifestyle. Having a keen interest in beer, wines, spirits and hookahs, he has spent years on learning and experiments on a variety of alcohol and hookahs worldwide. Through his books he passed his knowledge to entrepreneur investors, businessman etc. to help them take the experience to next level.

Read more at https://www.mindpop.in.

MINDPOP

About the Publisher

MindPop© is an international publication with readers and contributors from across the globe.

It is a platform for every new writer. You can write? We can publish.

It is a hub for a reader of various genres.

MindPop© offers EBook design and distribution. Deal with one entity for all your book publishing needs. We also have a team of expert book marketers who can provide you with a marketing plan check and optimise meta-data, help you encourage reviewers to review your book online, help you get going with promoting your book on social media etc

MindPop© also offers services in editing, illustration, cover design and marketing, meaning that we can cover all the requirements of our customers.

Our mission: To empower writers, businesses and organisations to distribute high quality EBooks throughout the world.

Our promise to you: We will be flexible, authentic and supportive to you or your organisation's unique needs.

MindPop© Experts With our combined knowledge of publishing and EBook technology, we are positioned to help you succeed. There are complexities in EBook and print (and print on demand) production that DIY-authors and many self-publishing businesses are not geared to cope with, especially the fast-changing nature of technology. However, our aim is to guide and support you to achieve your publishing goals.

To sum up, we're where you would enter for a casual stroll but walk out with an ignited mind.

We're food for thought. We're soup for your soul. We're MindPoP!

APR 2020

OCT 2020

CPSIA information can be obtained
at www.ICGtesting.com
Printed in the USA
LVHW111526181020
669091LV00003B/604

9 781393 555438